HOLINESS

the journey, the joy, the difference

HOLINESS

the journey, the joy, the difference

TOM HERMIZ

BEACON HILL PRESS
OF KANSAS CITY

ISBN-13: 978-0-8341-2131-7
ISBN-10: 0-8341-2131-X

Library of Congress Cataloging-in-Publication Data
Hermiz, Tom, 1938-
Holiness : the journey, the joy, the difference / by Tom Hermiz.
p. cm.
ISBN 0-8341-2131-X (pbk.)
1. Holiness—Christianity. I. Title.

BT767.H47 2004
234'.8—dc22
2004003225

10 9 8 7 6 5 4 3 2

Contents

1

Holiness Makes a Personal Difference

Thomas was an Assyrian born in Midyat, Turkey. When he was 5 years old the Muslims in that part of the world were on another of their many "Jihads," or "Holy Wars." They were determined to eradicate Christianity from the Middle East. Thomas's father, Emanuel, formed a small army trying to defend the Christians in his area. Because of his efforts, a price was put on his head, and after he was ambushed several times his family and friends insisted that he escape to the United States. He left for the States, planning to get settled before sending for his family. Tragically, before he could send for them, the Muslims invaded Midyat. In that horrific battle Emanuel's wife, mother, and 28 other family members died as martyrs for their Christian faith.

At 5 years old, Thomas was not killed, but instead a Muslim soldier picked him up off the street and took him home to raise him as a Muslim. For the next 4 years Thomas was passed around from one home to another until one of his uncles finally found him and smuggled him out of the country. Thomas crossed the ocean and was reunited with Emanuel, the father he didn't even remember. Thomas grew into a troubled, rage-filled teenager. He lived for the day he could return to Turkey and kill the people who murdered his mother and so many other members of his family.

Emanuel and Thomas lived next door to a couple who both taught Sunday School. That couple saw the pain and rage in Thomas and invited him into their home and to their church. Thomas responded to their love, and one night he knelt by his bed and asked God to come into his heart and help him to be a good person. Thomas's life was powerfully changed that night.

In the months that followed, Thomas continued to struggle with anger and bitterness toward those who were the instruments of such cruelty when he was a youngster. Thomas was 17 years old when he heard the message of holiness for the first time, and he immediately realized that he needed this deeper work of grace. He was the first one to the altar that evening, seeking the experience of entire sanctification. He struggled with bitterness and revenge, but that night he surrendered everything to God and asked Him to set him free from unholy attitudes and deliver him from the awful rage he was trying to suppress. When Thomas got up from the altar the bitterness and desire for revenge were gone. He had a new passion—to return to Turkey and find those who had massacred his family so he could share the love of Christ with them. As an adult Thomas returned to the Middle East as often as possible to share the love of Christ with as many people as possible. Thomas was so powerfully changed by God's sanctifying grace that he never displayed carnal attitudes or actions in his life. He was always kind, calm, and loving. It was a remarkable change in one who had once struggled with such rage and hatred.

Thomas eventually married and became a pastor, and at 82 years of age he and his wife made their last trip to Turkey. During their return flight to the States, a Muslim sat next to them on the plane. For six hours Thomas shared his personal story and the gospel message with this Muslim man. He was just about to ask him if he could pray with him to accept Christ as Savior when the Muslim man turned toward Thomas and said, "Sir, you have been telling me about Jesus Christ and now I want to invite Him into my heart. Will you pray with me?" Thomas then led the man in the sinner's prayer. Just two years later Thomas died, but this event on the plane was one of the great thrills of all his years in walking with the Lord.

Thomas was a sanctified man who lived a consistent and victorious Christian life. Thomas was also my father, so I was blessed to be born into a family with godly parents who set a wonderful example. When I was still quite young my mother shared with me that while she was still expecting me God revealed to her that she was carrying a son who would preach the gospel. I was genuinely excited about the prospect of growing up and becoming a preacher—so much so that from time to time I stood on the milk box on the front porch and preached to the people walking up and down the street. It was great fun to remind people they should get right with God or they would burn in hell.

But in my teen years I rebelled against God and began to pursue the things of the world. After I graduated from high school the parents of the girl I was dating invited me to go to Canada with them for vacation. I quickly accepted the invitation for two reasons. First of all, it meant I could spend more time with my girlfriend. Second, the trip was the same week as our annual church camp meeting at Lilly Lake, New York. I wanted to get as far away from the camp as I could because I didn't want to risk falling under conviction. I knew that if I got saved, it would change all of my carefully made plans to do what I wanted to do. I had been accepted by my chosen college and planned to major in music. My goal was to someday make it big in the world of jazz music with my trumpet.

I was in Canada for only a few days when my girlfriend and I suddenly couldn't stand each other. Whatever we thought we had going was suddenly gone. I was miserable, she was miserable, and her parents were miserable. I woke up early one morning and decided to hitchhike from Canada to my home in Endicott, New York. The first car that drove up was a brand-new black Cadillac. The driver asked me where I was going. When I told him he said, "Well, get in, because that's where I'm headed." He was an IBM executive based in Endicott, and he took me all the way to my front door. At first I thought this was just my good luck. Later I learned that my mother and a group of ladies at the camp were praying for God to bring me home and to the camp and to an altar of prayer.

Early Saturday morning I drove to the campground and found a bed in the dorm where I expected to get a few hours of sleep. At 10:30 A.M. the morning service began, and the singing woke me. I got dressed and went over to the tabernacle and sat down on the back row. The evangelist that morning was Rev. Dorothy Meadows, and although I think I was the only sinner in that small Saturday service, she was pouring out her heart with tears and great compassion. I was deeply convicted and realized I needed God. When she gave the invitation she came back to where I was standing and invited me to go forward to the altar and pray. Drawn by the Holy Spirit, I followed her down the aisle and asked God to save me. I sensed how lost I really was and cried out to God for mercy. He heard my prayers, forgave me of my sins, and saved me on the last Saturday of July in 1956.

My life changed that morning, and I have never been the same since. When I got up from the altar, one of the most beautiful girls I had ever seen said to me, "You don't know me, but your sister and I have been praying for your salvation this whole year. Now," she said, "why don't you come to Circleville Bible College for at least a year and really get grounded in your spiritual life."

I looked at her and thought that if all the girls at that college were as beautiful as she, it must be a pretty good school. It was love at first sight. I immediately changed my plans and enrolled there for college. Within five months we were engaged, then married the following June.

During my freshman year I sensed my need for God's sanctifying grace. Late one night I was alone on the athletic field, searching my heart and seeking God. I struggled with a couple of things. First of all, I knew God had called me to preach, and every preacher I had ever known up to that point seemed to be living at the poverty level. I had been poor all of my life and was tired of it. I wanted to make money and even told God that if He would let me have a secular job, I would give generously and work hard in a local church. The second issue I struggled with was the fear that if I surrendered my all to God, He might want me to be a missionary. Missionaries had stayed in my home on a regular basis when I was growing up, and I had listened with rapt attention as they talked about wild animals, snakes, and scorpions. As a little boy I had a phobia of dogs, so the thought of being a missionary was terrifying to me.

But that night on the athletic field as I prayed for God's sanctifying grace I came to the place where my hunger for a pure heart and my desire to please God was stronger than my fears, even if it meant poverty. I decided that if He would go with me, I would do whatever He wanted me to do and go wherever He wanted me to go. I asked God to deliver me from my awful self-centeredness, cleanse all the rebellion from my heart, and fill me with His Holy Spirit. When I said a complete yes to the whole will of God, tremendous peace and joy filled my heart. My life has never been the same since that night.

I confess that there have been times when my performance hasn't measured up. When that happens I ask for God's forgiveness, and He has always met my need. Over the years He has revealed blind spots and inconsistencies in my life, giving me new insights and light. It has always been my joy to receive this light and be obedient to God. After consecration and cleansing it has been a daily walk of growing in the grace and knowledge of our Lord and Savior Jesus Christ.

Today I serve as a full-time evangelist with my denomination. Although God did not call me to the mission field, He did give me the wonderful privilege of serving for 22 years as the president of a missionary-sending mission board. I have not lived in poverty because the Lord has more than abundantly met my needs.

2

The Great Commandment Is a Life of Love

Hearing that Jesus had silenced the Sadducees, the Pharisees got together. One of them, an expert in the law, tested him with this question: "Teacher, which is the greatest commandment in the Law?" Jesus replied, "'Love the Lord your God with all your heart and with all your soul and with all your mind.' This is the first and greatest commandment. And the second is like it: 'Love your neighbor as yourself.' All the Law and the Prophets hang on these two commandments" (Matt. 22:34-40).

Love is a four-letter word with more than one meaning. You may have heard about the young man who was proposing marriage to his girlfriend and started by saying, "I'm not rich and I don't have a hot sports car or a fancy speedboat like Jerome, but I do love you." His girlfriend replied, "Well, I love you too, but tell me a little more about Jerome."

Unfortunately many persons in our society have never experienced anything more than a shallow, fickle, superficial kind of love. In the above passage from Matthew, Christ gives us a wonderful lesson in love. A legal expert—a lawyer—came to Him and asked Him the kind of question you would expect a lawyer to ask, "Which is the greatest commandment in the Law?" Jesus replied, "'Love the Lord your God with all your heart and with all your soul and with all your mind.' This is the first and greatest commandment. And the second is like it: 'Love your neighbor as yourself.' All the Law and the Prophets hang on these two commandments" (Matt. 22:35-40). Loving God with all of your heart and loving your neighbor as yourself are the very essence of holiness of heart and life.

John tells us that to love God with our whole heart means "you will obey what I command" (John 14:15). Jesus said something similar when He said, "If anyone loves me, he will obey my teaching" (v. 23). This is the practical side of living a holy life. To love God is to know His commandments and to keep them. It might be easier to talk about our love for God in terms of an emotional response to Him, but the love that God desires is a love that is expressed in wholehearted, day by day, consistent obedience to His will. This is what the Bible refers to as *agape* love—the kind of love God has for us. Agape love is not primarily an emotional kind of love but rather a *volitional* kind of love that is completely spiritual. It is love that acts out of the reservoir that God is to our souls.

Another word for love that is used in the New Testament is *philos*—the kind of love that might be felt between friends. Strong emotion is attached to this kind of love, and it is the warm feeling you get for people you really like and enjoy being around. It is nearly impossible to command this love because emotions are so heavily tied to it. Our love for God may include great emotion from time to time, but God is far more interested in something deeper and more substantial than an emotional response.

Loving God impacts every area of your life. It affects your values, your priorities, your stewardship, your relationships, and your vocation. It is a wonderful feeling to worship God and to sing with great emotion "Oh, How I Love Jesus," but God is most interested in how you carry out your love for Him in your day-to-day life. This does not mean that there is no place for emotion in our worship. Our emotions are a gift from God. But God is interested in your character—honesty, integrity, and morality. He is more concerned about you showing your love for Him in the use of your finances, your observation of the Sabbath, the way you use His name, and the keeping of His commandments. God already knows your heart without the veil of emotion.

To love God in this manner will require you to surrender everything to His Lordship and allow Him to cleanse your heart from sin. Self-interest and selfish ambition have no place in the heart of one who is filled with the Holy Spirit and living a holy life. The true demonstration of your love for God is not revealed in emotional worship in the sanctuary. Rather, it is revealed in the way you obey Him daily.

When Jesus commanded "love your neighbor as yourself" (Matt. 22:39) He was not referring to the *philos* kind of love. Jesus wasn't talking about liking people in the same way you "like" your friends and your family. He used the word *agape* in this passage. Jesus meant that if we truly love Him and endeavor to live a holy life, we will seek to treat persons as He would treat them. How they deserve to be treated doesn't matter. Whether or not we feel like it, we should try to treat them right and seek to preserve their lives in the same manner we seek to preserve our own lives.

If you are hungry, you eat. If you are cold, you seek shelter in a warm house or under a cozy blanket. If you are tired, you think about where to find some rest. Jesus commanded us in Matt. 22:39 to treat others as we would treat ourselves—to love others as we love ourselves. But Jesus did not stop there. He also commanded us to love our enemies. That does not mean that we will feel warm and fuzzy about our enemies but that through the power of the Holy Spirit we can forgive them "seventy-seven times" (18:22), turn the other cheek (5:39), and go the second mile (v. 41). We can willfully refuse to seek revenge. We can determine by the power of the Holy Spirit to always seek the highest good. We should be as sensitive to the needs of others as we are to our own needs. This means loving people we don't even like! We may not like their personality, temperament, lifestyle, habits, or the things they say and do, but by God's grace it is possible to treat them right.

It was Saturday evening in Columbus, Ohio, and I was preaching at a missions conference. I anticipated a good night's rest because I was to preach three times Sunday morning beginning at 8:15. When I settled into bed I realized that there was a party going on in the room right next door.

Besides the raucous laughter and loud talking, I could hear profanity and cans snapping open. At about 15 minutes before one o'clock I was still wide awake, so I called the front desk. "The people in the room next door are having a party and it's nearly one o'clock. I have to preach at 8:15 A.M., and I need to get a few hours' sleep. Is there anything you can do?" They were very apologetic and said, "We'll call them."

A few minutes later I heard the phone ring in the room next door and someone say, "Hello." When they hung up the phone somebody in the room said, "Who was it? What did they want?"

"Oh, that was the front desk and they said we are making too much noise and keeping people awake and that we ought to quiet down."

They laughed. About 3 A.M. they finally quieted down. I fell asleep, and at 4:45 my alarm sounded. I rolled out of bed, put my feet on the floor, and thought about turning the television up as loud as it would go. You know, just to let them know morning had broken and it was time to get up! But immediately I realized that I should treat them the way I wish they had treated me. I tried to be quiet and did my best not to wake them. When I finished getting ready for my busy day and walked out of my room I listened for a moment, and they were still snoring. What a temptation to slam the door! But I didn't. I remembered, "Do to others what you would have them do to you" (Matt. 7:12). When I walked past their door I had peace in my heart and in my mind. As I finished preaching the third service I felt as good as I had when I began preaching in the first service.

A holy life is reflected in the way we treat and respond to others. We no longer seek revenge against those who have wronged us but instead seek to be a blessing to them. Loving others with an agape love allows us to kindle a desire in others to know Jesus as we know Him. Agape love is not an emotional flurry but a principle by which we live that orders and directs every facet of our lives. Agape love allows us to show unconditional and unselfish concern for others. It is love that transcends all barriers.

Sin can be described as love gone astray or love that has been misdirected and distorted. It is a perversion of Christian love. Sin is at its essence idolatry and is what happens when anyone or anything besides the living God takes ownership of one's life.

God gives us complete freedom to choose whom we will serve. Sometimes people are consumed with themselves or become extremely prideful. Others may place so much value on another person, such as a spouse or loved one, that they make a particular relationship the center of their lives. For others it is a philosophy or ambition. What is the supreme affection of your heart and life?

Charles Allen, in his book *The Holy Spirit,* tells the story of a country boy named John. John was raised by his mother, and she was the only person he loved. He didn't think he could love anyone else. One day someone introduced him to the prettiest girl he had ever seen. Eventually they were married, and John's capacity for love was increased; now he loved two people. It wasn't long until the young man's love was once more stretched to enjoy the arrival of his first child, a precious baby girl. Then one day someone introduced him to Jesus Christ, and when John fell in love with Jesus something dramatic happened. He suddenly discovered that he had the capacity to love everybody.

We can be so deeply in love with the Master that the horizon of that love will extend to every person we meet. If we love our neighbors, we are not going to harm them in any way. We will actively endeavor to do as much good as we possibly can. That is how we know that Christian love is greater and stronger than emotional love.

A man from Ohio was a true prayer warrior who was awake at 4 A.M. every morning to pray.

He was short in stature, and his prayer list was longer than he was tall. He prayed for every person, every institution, and every need on his list. He spent hours each day in intercessory prayer. One Sunday night during church he noticed a large man with a ruddy complexion in the back of the church who retained a cud of tobacco in his jaw. At the invitation at the end of the service he felt impressed to invite the large man to the altar. When he spoke to the stranger about giving his heart to God, it so infuriated the large man that he spit tobacco juice in his face. The shorter man reached into his pocket, pulled out his handkerchief, and wiped off the stinking mess. He then looked at the man and said, "Sir, I love you, and I will be praying for you every day that you will give your heart to Jesus."

Months later a citywide camp meeting was held in the local auditorium. The weather was stormy that night and the musicians were running late. Since the service was going to get a late start, those in charge decided to ask people who were already gathered there if anyone would like to share his or her testimony. Halfway back in the auditorium a large man with a ruddy complexion stood. "I want to testify because I have been one of the meanest, vilest sinners in this part of the country. In fact, I was so mean that several months ago I happened to be in church for the first time with my wife. A short man offered to pray with me at the altar, but instead I spat my tobacco juice into his face. That was the turning point in my life, because he said, 'I love you, and I will be praying for you every day that you will give your heart to Jesus.' I could tell he meant it. I could tell it wasn't just words. I saw it in his eyes.

"I'm a truck driver and every day on the highway, every time I heard my wheels turn, all I could hear was that man's voice saying, 'Sir, I love you, and I'm praying for you to give your heart to Jesus.' Every night I laid down my head in some cheap motel beside the road and I would see his face in my dreams radiating the love of Jesus, saying, 'Sir, I love you.' A few weeks ago, I couldn't stand it any longer. I pulled my truck to the side of the road, called my wife, and told her I would be home soon and to get the preacher to be there when I arrived. I told her I wanted to get right with God. When I got home the preacher was there, and along with my wife, I knelt at the couch in the living room, repented of my sins, and gave my heart to the Lord. I don't know who that man was or where he is, but I hope that someday he will get the message that because of his love for Jesus and his genuine love for me, I am now a child of God."

Down on the front row a quiet, unassuming,

short man slightly lifted his hands to heaven and softly said, "Thank you, Jesus. I got the message."

What kind of message is your life sending to those around you? Can others see how much you love God? Can they see the love God has planted in you?

3

The Believer's Most Urgent Need

It is impossible to live a Christian life without the Holy Spirit. Jesus knew this when He commanded His disciples:

> *"Do not leave Jerusalem, but wait for the gift my Father promised, which you have heard me speak about. For John baptized with water, but in a few days you will be baptized with the Holy Spirit." So when they met together, they asked him, "Lord, are you at this time going to restore the kingdom to Israel?" He said to them: "It is not for you to know the times or dates the Father has set by his own authority. But you will receive power when the Holy Spirit comes on you; and you will be my witnesses in Jerusalem, and in all Judea and Samaria, and to the ends of the earth." After he said this, he was taken*

> *up before their very eyes, and a cloud hid him from their sight* (Acts 1:4-9).

As Jesus shared His final message to His disciples He chose His words very carefully. The promise of the Father that Jesus referred to stems from Ezek. 36:27 when the prophet says God would "put my Spirit in you." But before that could occur Jesus intervened and said, "Don't even think about going out and doing ministry. Don't even think about going out to preach. Don't even think about going out and trying to cast out demons. You are not ready!" That is remarkable when you think about the fact that He had been preparing them for ministry for more than three years. They had heard every sermon, walked beside Him along every mile of the way, and watched Him perform many miracles. They had the opportunity and the time to ask Him thousands of questions over those three years. But not one of the questions they asked could prepare them for what Jesus knew they needed most. He knew they needed to be filled with the Holy Spirit for the Church to survive. There is no person who is so talented, so resourceful, so educated that he or she can minister without the filling of the Holy Spirit.

It's tempting to look at the church today and think that we're only one pithy mission statement away from winning the world for Christ. Or, we think, maybe a better organization structure is the answer—or a better administrative team—or more precise goal setting. I appreciate the importance of having all of these important tools. But not one of these tools—nor a combination of all of them—will make any difference in the direction of your church if its people are not filled with the Holy Spirit.

I remember attending a ministerial convention several years ago where a pastor from one of the largest churches in America was invited to speak. He came into the gathering of preachers from a different theological persuasion and said, "Gentlemen, your problem is your doctrine. If you could get your doctrine straightened out, you could really accomplish something." Doctrine is not the problem.

Others think worship style is the key. Are we traditional or contemporary? What ratio of hymns to choruses should we sing? Should we sing out of hymnals or from a screen on the wall? If we were as particular about the condition of our own spiritual walk as we are about the color of our hymnbooks, we could make a great impact in this world!

Jesus knew that His newly commissioned disciples would never make a difference in their world without the Holy Spirit living in them. As the writer of Acts confirms, the disciples of the Gospel narratives tell us that they did exactly as Jesus directed them to do. They stayed in Jerusalem in a secluded, secret room in constant prayer. Had they been impatient and hurried away to practice what they had learned, they would not have been where God could bless them with the Holy Spirit. Without the Holy Spirit, the Church itself would not exist.

We may sometimes be tempted to substitute legalism and emotionalism for the Holy Spirit. The disciples did not settle for a substitute. They secluded themselves and removed all the distractions from their lives that would interfere with concentrating on receiving the promise of the Father. Sometimes today we are tempted to follow religious fads.

Not the disciples. They came together of one heart and mind to seek God's will for their impending ministries. They did not come together to eat or to grumble about what was wrong in the world around them. They wanted the Holy Spirit more than they wanted food, more than they wanted fellowship, more than they wanted air to breathe, more than life itself.

Do you have that intensity in your life, your church, your community?

In Acts 2 God answered their prayers. "When the day of Pentecost came, they were all together in one place. . . . All of them were filled with the Holy Spirit" (vv. 1, 4). This is the fulfillment of a thousand-year-old prophecy. But, even more, it is a promise of God to the Church—that everyone can be filled with the Holy Spirit. He's available, He's ready, and He's willing to dwell within us. We hold the key.

Why is the indwelling of the Holy Spirit so crucial in a believer's heart? When the disciples were filled, they first experienced the purification of their hearts. Many in holiness circles shy away from emphasizing this step of heart purification, but I believe it is crucial. Over the past 22 years I have interviewed thousands of young men and women who felt the call of God to mission service. Most of them attended holiness-tradition colleges and had been raised in holiness churches. They understood the concept of being filled with the Holy Spirit, but many of them knew nothing about heart purity.

I explained it to them like this: When a believer is born again by the grace of God, his or her sins and willful transgressions are blotted out—all is forgiven. That person is a new creation in Jesus Christ, and the Holy Spirit enables him or her to live a Christian life. However, there is still a condition that exists in this new believer's heart called carnality. The carnal heart is one that continues to pursue the pleasures of the world rather than seeking the Holy Spirit's influence. Carnality and spirituality are continually in conflict. Carnality is rooted out, and the Holy Spirit is free to move within the believer when he or she becomes sanctified through a second work of grace.

Peter stands in Acts 15 and declares the Gentiles were filled with the Holy Spirit. "God . . . made no distinction between us and them, for he purified their hearts by faith" (vv. 8-9).

Heart purity is an extremely important step for a believer. The psalmist wrote, "Who may ascend the hill of the Lord? Who may stand in his holy place? He who has clean hands and a pure heart" (24:3-4). When Jesus preached the Sermon on the Mount, He said, "Blessed are the pure in heart, for they will see God" (Matt. 5:8). You can have a pure heart—you need a pure heart—so that your motives and intentions will be pure.

Second, those assembled in the Upper Room received power. Jesus said, "But you will receive power when the Holy Spirit comes on you; and you will be my witnesses in Jerusalem, and in all Judea and Samaria, and to the ends of the earth" (Acts 1:8). After those in the Upper Room were filled with the Holy Spirit, they began to teach, witness, and preach with power. Thousands were saved, and the world was changed. There was no organizational structure, no church building, no mission statement, and very little money.

But the believers in the Early Church had received the Holy Spirit. They had the *power* of God at work in their lives. You can be filled with the Holy Spirit and have power over the pressures and temptations of the world. The power of the Holy Spirit will help you rise above the materialism that permeates our society. The Holy Spirit will give you power to reject the messages of sexual permissiveness that crowd the airwaves. You will have the power to witness about the presence of the Holy Spirit in your life.

Dwight Moody was short, stocky, with little formal education, and is noted in part for his butchering of the English language. His initial writing was an embarrassment to everyone who knew him because his writing skills were so poor. Despite these impediments, he is believed to have preached the gospel to more than 100 million people during his lifetime in the 19th century. Rev. Moody had in his church two little old ladies who perceived that he had not been filled by the Holy Spirit. Upon leaving church each week, they would warmly shake his hand and say to him, "Pastor Moody, we're praying for you. We're praying that you'll be filled with the Holy Spirit."

It was irritating to Moody to think that these ladies were praying that their pastor would be filled with the Holy Spirit. Every Sunday when he preached, after just a few words, these two little ladies would look at each other, and they would shake their heads—they knew their prayers had not been answered.

One day in 1871 Moody was walking down Wall Street in New York City when he became overwhelmed by his own desperate need for the Holy Spirit. He was tired of the barrenness in his ministry. As he walked, he cried out to God, and suddenly his prayer was answered. God poured out His Spirit upon Dwight Moody. Moody later recounted he ran back to his hotel room where he lay prostrate on the floor, filled and laden with the presence of God. Finally he asked God to stop, for the glory was more than he could bear!

Moody returned to his home church to preach, and after being in the pulpit for only a couple of minutes, he looked down to find the two little ladies smiling and nodding their heads in affirmation—their prayers had been answered. Their pastor was filled with the Spirit! Estimated to have been responsible for bringing more than 1 million souls to Christ before the microphone was invented, Moody said, "I preached the same sermons, but now there was a difference. Now there was a fruitfulness and effectiveness. Now there was poignant conviction and now people were responding and coming to Christ."

The most desperate need of the church today is

to be filled with the Spirit of God. Many years ago while holding a revival in Minnesota, I discovered that the pastor and his wife were on the verge of burnout—complete nervous exhaustion. There was so much discord, disagreement, and fussing in that church that it was taking a physical toll on the couple.

One night, one of the ladies in the church invited her neighbor to come and attend the service. The neighbor lady was an active member of another church in town and had never been in a holiness church before. My sermon that night was a very simple one on entire sanctification that answered the basic questions: What is it? What will it do for you? What will it not do to you? When I gave the invitation, the neighbor was the first person to the altar.

When I stepped down to pray with her, her sincerity was unquestionable. She witnessed to the work God was doing in her. "I've been a member of my church all of my life. I love Jesus, and I love the Word of God. I try to do everything my church asks of me and have tried to live a Christian life." She continued, "I sat here tonight, and I'd never heard this truth before in my life. It was brand-new to me. But as you went through the message, the Spirit of the Lord kept bearing witness to my heart that this was for me. He promised that if I would seek Him,

He would indeed fill me with His Holy Spirit. Although I'd never heard it before, there was this witness and this warmth in my heart that I knew it was true, and I knew it was what I was hungry for. He is not only my Savior but also my Sanctifier. He has filled me with His Spirit!"

You can have the assurance that you have been filled with the Holy Spirit. If you are born again, and if you are a child of God, you are a candidate for His infilling. All you need do is surrender to His call upon your life, and He will fill you and purify your heart.

4

Free at Last

But now that you have been set free from sin and have become slaves to God, the benefit you reap leads to holiness, and the result is eternal life (Rom. 6:22).

Alexander was a Russian physicist who decided at the age of 26 that he could no longer tolerate the oppression of communism. So, equipped with only a backpack, he set off on foot toward the northwest border of the Soviet Union. His goal was to reach Sweden and freedom. However, to get there he would have to cross some of the most rugged terrain in Eastern Europe. After 23 days and 23 nights—his body, mind, and nerves stretched to the breaking point—Alexander finally reached his goal. He was free. A short time later he wrote to a friend describing his journey, "The sense of freedom exhilarates me constantly in my new life."

Have you ever felt the exhilaration of being free? Just as Alexander was born under the oppression of communism, we are all born under the oppressive tyranny of sin. Like that brave young physicist, however, we need not continue living under sin's domination. You can be free from sin! Paul was clear in his letter to the Romans that we can be free from slavery to sin when he declared, "But now that you have been set free from sin . . . the benefit you reap leads to holiness, and the result is eternal life" (6:22).

The first thing we must do is believe freedom is possible. I am constantly amazed at the number of people who continue to teach and believe that it is impossible to live their lives free from sin. These naysayers claim that everyone sins a little bit and that it happens every day in one way or another. This teaching is so prevalent that many people have accepted it without stopping to discern whether or not it has any biblical support. Is that what Scripture says? Do you believe that you are doomed to live a life of constant frustration, failing to please God every day?

Not at all! God makes it clear that we can be set free from the power of sin now. Not tomorrow, not next month, not next year, but right now you can be free from sin. Paul also wrote, "Count yourselves dead to sin but alive to God in Christ Jesus" (Rom. 6:11). Your first step in finding this freedom is to understand that you are a slave to sin, but God can set you free.

When we are born, we are each infected by sin. We enter this world as slaves to sin; it is the dominating force in our lives. Before we ever learn the difference between right and wrong, something within us rebels and says *no* to authority. Like selfish children, we begin to say, "I'm going to do it my way, not your way." We are willing to be deceitful or harm others to get what we want.

Think back to when you were a child, or think of children you know. The tendency toward sin is obvious in children. You don't have to teach a child to lie. Most of the time it's a struggle to teach a youngster to tell the truth. You will never struggle to teach a child to be selfish—it comes naturally. The challenge will be to teach a child to share. You will not have to teach a child to disobey—it is respect for authority that must be instilled. That is because each of us enters this world with a heart that is bent toward evil. We are born separated from God, living under condemnation.

But Jesus provides freedom. Thank God there is a remedy for the sickness of sin. God provided a means of deliverance from all sin through His Son

Jesus Christ. The Bible says in 2 Cor. 5:21, "God made him who had no sin to be sin for us, so that in him we might become the righteousness of God."

The Bible also teaches that if we come to Christ and repent of our sins, consecrating our lives to Him, there is both forgiveness for sin and cleansing from sin. When we repent of our sins, we are forgiven for our disobedient acts of sin. And when we are sanctified, God cleanses our hearts from our inborn *tendency* to sin.

Thus Paul was prompted to say that we should not be slaves to sin any longer. We now have a choice about whether or not sin will rule our hearts and lives. Because of what Jesus did for us on the Cross Paul wrote in Rom. 6:22, "But now that you have been set free from sin," and in 8:1, "Therefore, there is now no condemnation for those who are in Christ Jesus." Jesus sets us free from sin.

Paul realized he had a sin problem and searched in vain for ways to get away from his internal desire to sin. First he tried culture. The result was that he became a cultured sinner. Next he tried education. With all of his education Paul was still just a cultured, educated sinner. Finally, Paul thought that religion was the answer. He was known as a strict and pietistic Jew and followed Judaism to the letter. This dedication still did not save him.

Perhaps you have tried various remedies for

your sin and have found that none of them work—not culture, not education, not morality, not philosophy, and not religion. Your *inner nature* remains unchanged. At best, these remedies only give you the *appearance* of being a better person. Paul summed it up in Rom. 8:3 when he said, "What the law was powerless to do in that it was weakened by the sinful nature, God did by sending his own Son in the likeness of sinful man." Only Christ can set us free from sin. He can do for us what we cannot do for ourselves through our own actions. He forgives our sin and purifies our hearts. The God who spoke the world into existence and shaped humanity from the dust of the earth can deliver us from sin's grip. We must not settle for less.

Many Christians feel sin is inevitable, but Scripture does not support this philosophy. It is a low expectation that becomes a self-fulfilling prophecy; we expect to sin, and so we do.

John wrote, "He who does what is sinful is of the devil . . . No one who is born of God will continue to sin . . . because he has been born of God" (1 John 3:8-9). That tells me that a born-again believer does not have to practice sin or continue to willfully disobey God.

The retired president of a leading seminary was bemoaning the spiritual condition of many recent graduates who would soon take their places in ministry across the country. He said, "They have drug problems, alcohol problems, tobacco problems, and sexual problems . . . most of them do not have anything closely resembling a quiet time with the Lord. These are the ones going out to fill our pulpits."

I believe that sad commentary on the spiritual condition of the leaders of our churches is the direct result of a watered-down gospel. We have not been lifting the cross of Jesus and assuming the power that is in His blood to change us. Of course, it is possible that even a sanctified believer would yield to temptation and commit sin. This side of heaven we are not free from the *possibility* of sin, but we can be free from the *power* of sin.

What is the condition of your life today? Have you been set free from sin? Your first step in answering yes is to believe that God can do what nothing and no one else can—change your heart.

I'm a fan of Snoopy and Charlie Brown, the characters created by Charles Schulz. I remember seeing one of his comic strips in a newspaper in which the children are all gathered on the baseball field choosing sides for their upcoming game. One child has a long, very sad-looking face because he has never been chosen. However, this day, someone yells his name across the playground, "Chaarrlie Broowwnn!" Charlie Brown jumps to his feet and skips down the baseline to join his new teammates, and the caption reads: "Happiness is being chosen to play on the team."

The Bible says that we have been chosen for something far more wonderful than a baseball team; we have been chosen for holiness. It is God's will for you to be holy and free from sin. Accepting that freedom will require an act of your will in response to God's call, but only you can make the choice to be completely consecrated to Him.

One of the most comforting messages in the Bible is that God has chosen us to be His children. The Bible teaches that before the foundation of the world was laid, God set you apart for himself and determined that you should be holy as He is holy (see Eph. 1:4 and 1 Pet. 1:16).

Undoubtedly you have felt the call of God on your life at some point. He called to you, and His grace prompted you to seek forgiveness. It was God who made you feel the weight of your sin. He drew your mind to himself through the Holy Spirit because He loves you and has chosen you. He wants you to be free from the guilt of sin.

God not only wants to save you from sin but also continues to call you to holiness. He wants to free you from the power of sin.

Do you ever feel dissatisfied with the way you

are and long to be a better person? That's the grace of God at work in your heart and mind. Have you ever wanted to cry to the Lord, "Lord, please change me"? It is God who put that desire in your heart so that He could release you and make you a different person. God is concerned not only with the things you do but also with who you are. He has called you into a wonderful relationship with Him, and as His child you can reflect His character in every way. How does it feel to know that God has planned something so wonderful with you in mind?

In his poem "The Road Not Taken" Robert Frost wrote, "Two roads diverged in a wood and I, I took the one less traveled by, and that has made all the difference." Each of us makes hundreds of choices every day—some more important than others. When God asks us to follow Him, we make a decision—a choice—to serve Him. If we choose to serve ourselves rather than God, we are really choosing sin. Remember—in our *natural condition* we are slaves to sin. Sadly, people regularly choose sin and live under the domination of their own selfishness and become greedy and materialistic or secluded and alienated from true friendships. The results of making the wrong choice are monumental. If we choose self and sin, we are separated from God. If we choose to follow God, we can become holy and free and bask in the promise of eternal life in His presence.

Have you made this choice in your life?

God made it possible for you to choose life when He went to the Cross in your place, but that doesn't make the choice an easy one. In fact, I believe it would be impossible to choose God and leave behind our selfish desires and live a holy life under our own power. The good news is that we don't have to do it under our own power. God has given us the gift of His Holy Spirit to help us as we choose life.

You may have heard the story of the great concert pianist Ignacy Paderewski. One night as the concert hall filled with his admirers, the crowd buzzed with whispers of activity, everyone waiting for the great artist to come onstage and begin his performance. Suddenly a little five-year-old boy wiggled loose from his parents and climbed onto the stage. He had seen the concert grand piano and wanted to play it. Before his parents knew what was happening, the tyke was sitting on the bench. With one finger the boy began to plunk out the only song he knew: "Twinkle, Twinkle, Little Star." The audience burst into laughter, but the parents were embarrassed and humiliated as they frantically signaled to him to leave the stage. Then, calmly and with quiet composure, Paderewski himself appeared behind the boy and, leaning over, said, "Don't stop. Keep playing just as you are." And the great composer reached his long arms around the little fellow and improvised an accompaniment. In a few moments that simple tune turned into a concerto that filled the auditorium, bringing the audience to its feet in spontaneous applause. What a wonderful moment that must have been!

In the same way, the Holy Spirit helps us in our weaknesses. We couldn't do it on our own. But God—through His Holy Spirit—helps us. The Holy Spirit enables us to trust God for salvation. The Holy Spirit gives us the resolve to turn away from self and toward God. The Holy Spirit provides a way of escape when we are tempted and gives us the ability to turn the other cheek to our enemies and to love them.

Do you wonder how you could live up to the command of God to "be holy, because I am holy" (Lev. 11:44)? You can when the Holy Spirit lives *in* you.

Have you claimed this victory in your heart, or do you carry a burden of guilt because you know that you continue to sin? Based on the authority of God's Word, you can enjoy the knowledge that He will deliver you from all sin. By opening your heart to the cleansing work of the Holy Spirit, you can be free.

The Bible teaches that before the foundation of the world was laid, God set you apart for himself. He has called you to be holy. You can be free!

5

The Consecration of Sanctification

Therefore, I urge you, brothers, in view of God's mercy, to offer your bodies as living sacrifices, holy and pleasing to God—this is your spiritual act of worship. Do not conform any longer to the pattern of this world, but be transformed by the renewing of your mind. Then you will be able to test and approve what God's will is—his good, pleasing and perfect will (Rom. 12:1-2).

Karen fought and gasped for every breath. All the organs of her body were shutting down, and her life was slipping away. As her parents, Ella Mae and I waited in a small room down the hall from the intensive care unit. I prayed quietly, but I prayed as intensely as I have ever prayed. Suddenly, God took me back 22 years when Ella Mae and I stood in my father's church and I placed our baby, Karen, into his arms so he could lay his hands on her and bless her. As we dedicated Karen to the

Lord, we took our vows seriously. Even though she was of our flesh and blood, we recognized her as a gift from God. We covenanted with God to do our best to nurture her in the admonition of the Lord. We vowed to lead her to church and the means of grace as well as set an example that would make it easy for her to believe. We recognized that she was not ours to selfishly clutch to ourselves but that she belonged to God. We embraced our responsibility to be faithful stewards and loving parents.

Now Karen, extremely ill with meningitis, was in the final hours of her life. As I relived that precious occasion from 22 years earlier, I felt God questioning me. "Is she still Mine, or are you going to tell Me what to do and demand what you want? Are you going to leave her in My hands?"

All I could do was groan, it hurt so much. Finally I responded in prayer, "Lord, I can't fool You; You know my heart. You know exactly what I want You to do. I want You to go into that intensive care unit and put Your powerful hand upon her and heal her so we can walk out of this place with her. I know You can do that because I've watched You do it before. You are the Great Physician; it will not tax Your strength and power. Lord, that's exactly what I want You to do. But, Lord, I will not demand that You do what I want. You are Lord, You are God, and I know that You see the big picture and all I can see is this moment. You're a loving Heavenly Father, and You never make mistakes. I'm going to leave her in Your hands, and, Father, I'm just stepping back."

As I finished that prayer and turned to walk across the room and share with Ella Mae what I had just experienced, I looked out the doorway and saw two physicians come out of the intensive care unit and start down the hall. I knew why they were coming. I turned to Ella Mae and said, "The doctors are coming; I think it's over now." We held hands as they entered the room. The young physician who was in charge said some very kind words about our daughter and how hard they had tried everything they knew to do, then he broke into tears. That's when Ella Mae leaned forward and gently embraced him, saying, "Thank you, doctor. Thank you for caring; thank you for doing the best you could do. That's all we could ask of you, and now she is with the Lord and one day we will see her again."

With that she turned and laid her head on my shoulder, and we wept as we held each other as tightly as we've ever held each other. The hurt was so intense I felt physical pain. But what helped us the most during that traumatic and devastating time was that 22 years earlier we had *given* her to God.

Have you put your sons and daughters on the

altar of consecration? Have you reached the point where you have taken your hands off and said, "Lord, they're Yours, and I'm going to raise them for You and for Your glory"? Have you put your spouse, your marriage, your most beloved thing on the altar of consecration? Have you given Him your intellect, your personality, your sexuality, your gifts, your talents, your treasures, your time, your will? Have you given Him everything? Is He really Lord of your life? Unless He is Lord *of* all, He really isn't Lord *at* all. You'll have to make that 100 percent commitment in order to enjoy the fullness of His grace and Spirit in your heart and life. Consecrating your life to Him is your part in the work of grace called *entire sanctification.* It is then that He cleanses us from sin and fills us with His Holy Spirit.

Abraham's life is a powerful example of consecration. In Gen. 22:2, God said to Abraham, "Take your son, your only son, Isaac, whom you love, and go to the region of Moriah. Sacrifice him there as a burnt offering on one of the mountains I will tell you about."

Isaac was the son God promised Abraham and Sarah when they were long past childbearing age. He was a miracle—the avenue through which Abraham's seed would be multiplied. He would be the father of many nations. Now God was telling

Abraham to give him back and sacrifice him as a burnt offering.

Abraham got up early to do what God asked him to do. He took Isaac to the mountain, bound him, and placed him on the altar. Abraham was ready to take his son's life when God stopped him and provided a ram in the thicket to be used for the sacrifice. This event reveals Abraham's tremendous faith to believe that before God would go back on His promise He would raise Isaac from the dead if necessary. It also reveals Abraham's consecration to God. His complete surrender to God enabled him to be obedient. Our most precious possessions are gifts from God. Life, health, talents, family, and friends are treasures we must be willing to yield back to God if we are to live a holy life.

For believers who want God's best in their lives, consecration is more than just a spiritual exercise. Consecration is to the sanctified life what repentance is to the new birth. In the great plan of salvation God designed it so that there is a human side and a divine side. God will never do what we are supposed to do, but God must do what we cannot do. When we accept salvation, our part is repentance and no one else, not even God, can do that for us. It is God's part to forgive us, justify us, adopt us, and make us new in Christ Jesus. You could try for the rest of your life and you could never do that for yourself. It is the gift of God. In the sanctified life our part is the consecration. That means yielding and surrendering our will to the Lordship of Jesus Christ. No one else can do that for us. Then God's part is to cleanse our hearts from all sin and fill us with His love and Holy Spirit in the work of grace that we call entire sanctification.

If you desire to live a holy life and please God, consecration is much more than a routine, spiritual exercise. It is absolute, total abandonment of your will to the Lordship of Jesus Christ.

God requires 100 percent commitment—an absolute, unconditional yielding to His Lordship. It seems to me that many believers are about 99 percent committed. In this day of spiritual mediocrity where commitment to anything or anyone is not popular, 99 percent may seem like a lot. But if that 1 missing percent, that one thing, that one person, that one possession—even though it may seem perfectly legitimate—is more important to you than Christ is, it becomes an idol. That 1 percent can be a source of spiritual defeat in your life over and over again, and it will keep you from becoming the strong, fruitful Christian God wants you to be. Unless He is Lord *of* all, He isn't Lord *at* all.

By consecrating your life to God you allow Him to take complete control. Only one major issue is at stake: who is in control? Are you going to live according to God's will or according to your own will? Are you going to allow God to be God in your life, or are you going to play God?

God gives you complete freedom to do things your own way, so you can choose to say, "I'm not going to give up absolute control of my life to anyone for any reason. It's my life." But in spite of your competency to make decisions about your own life, your perspective is extremely limited compared to God's perspective. My daughter Karen's life was important to me, but my perspective was distorted by the emotions I felt as her father. Selfish ambitions and desires somehow affect your decisions unless your ultimate desire is to honor God. The challenge is to present ourselves to Him as living sacrifices and surrender all of our rights to Him. This is a consecration of your appetites—the natural, normal, God-given drives and hungers.

Today more than ever I find it necessary to lift my voice against other voices that tell us there are no absolutes and that everything is relative. God's absolutes are still relative and operating in today's postmodern society. If we put Him first in the appetites of our bodies, minds, and emotions, He can be Lord of our lives.

I learned a hard lesson when I was in junior high school. One Saturday night I was upstairs in my bedroom listening to a baseball game on the radio. My dad called to me that it was time to take a bath, and I responded to him, "All right, Dad. I will." I put the plug in the tub, turned on the water, and went back to my room to listen to the ninth inning of the game. During that ninth inning, someone hit a grand slam homer and tied up the game. It was the longest and most exciting game of the year! Sometime around the 14th or 15th inning my father came rushing up the stairs. That's when I noticed the water gushing down the stairway. I had forgotten to turn off the water, and it was spilling over and making an awful mess.

Similarly, filth and perversion running into your mind will eventually ruin something in your life. "For as he thinketh in his heart, so is he" (Prov. 23:7, KJV). With wickedness and immorality around us, we must constantly fill our minds with lovely, just, and pure things. When we do, His grace enables us to keep our lives clean and pure. Even when you are tempted to satisfy your natural desires in a manner contrary to the will of God, His grace will help you live a clean, pure life that glorifies Him.

Sometimes our personal ambitions lead us into dangerous territory. Have you given God your ambitions? You may rationalize that your ambitions are merely legitimate desires. Perhaps you believe that if you consecrate your all to God and put your life in His hands, He may send you to a hot, steamy jungle and make a missionary out of you, dumping you into a life of fun-free poverty. You may come up with all sorts of reasons for keeping control of your own life rather than turning it over to God. It is possible to come right to the point of consecrating your ambitions to God and then back away because you are unwilling to trust God more than you trust yourself. Satan will do his best to keep you from making this kind of commitment because he knows there is great power in a life that is completely consecrated to God.

Sometimes we are tripped up by our own self-centeredness. We want our own way, and we want it now! We like the dreams and plans we have for ourselves. God's agenda may upset our comfort zones. But whatever God requires, it is for your good and His glory. It may be hard to recognize when we're all wrapped up in the moment and the pressures of today, but our God knows best and wants us to come to the place where we are so committed to Him that we take our hands off and say, "Lord, my life is no longer my own. I will follow You wherever You lead."

When I was a teenager, there was a handful of girls in my high school that I thought were the most beautiful girls God ever made. I remember praying something like this: "Lord, I think she'd make a wonderful wife. I think it would be a wonderful thing if You'd just help her fall in love with me and we could get married." You know, sometimes the greatest blessings in life come about when God says no. It had been years since I'd been to my hometown, but I went back there and saw some of my old friends from high school. Some of those friends were the girls I had so adored as a teenager. When I think of my wonderful wife and realize how God provided her for me as one of the greatest blessings in my life, I know that He really does know best, regardless of what I think He should do in any given situation.

You may have some major concerns in your life today. If you seek God's guidance now and follow Him, it's likely that 10 or 20 years from now you'll look back and realize that seeking Him was the best thing you could have done. That takes a consecrated life.

God doesn't ask us to love our families or our friends any less when we consecrate our lives to Him, but He does require us to allow Him to be the primary affection of our hearts. He must be first in our lives. In fact, I've discovered that the more deeply you fall in love with Jesus, the greater your capacity is to love others. The love of God in our hearts brings us to the place of accountability and responsibility. We learn to treat people right instead of simply using them in a selfish way. We learn to give and to share and to respond to their needs and their desires.

It can become dangerous to allow our love for persons to compete with our love for God. Certainly I loved our daughter Karen and wanted to keep her on this earth, but giving her to God was an act of consecration.

When you consecrate your appetites, ambitions, and affections to Jesus Christ, He will truly be Lord of your life.

6

God's Part in the Cleansing

This is the message we have heard from him and declare to you: God is light; in him there is no darkness at all. If we claim to have fellowship with him yet walk in the darkness, we lie and do not live by the truth. But if we walk in the light, as he is in the light, we have fellowship with one another, and the blood of Jesus, his Son, purifies us from all sin. If we claim to be without sin, we deceive ourselves and the truth is not in us. If we confess our sins, he is faithful and just and will forgive us our sins and purify us from all unrighteousness. If we claim we have not sinned, we make him out to be a liar and his word has no place in our lives (1 John 1:5-10).

And so Jesus also suffered outside the city gate to make the people holy through his own blood (Heb. 13:12).

Because of the emphasis on scriptural holiness and entire sanctification, churches that are labeled as "holiness churches" have sometimes been accused of being theologically tangential. Nothing could be further from the truth. Holiness goes straight to the heart of the gospel. Sanctification is not a secondary matter but the very reason Jesus left heaven. His purpose for coming to earth was to pave the way for our sanctification.

God begins the process of making us holy when we repent of our sins and are saved. In theological terms we call this initial sanctification. Initial sanctification is followed by entire sanctification the moment we present ourselves to God as "living sacrifices" (Rom. 12:1). At that time of complete consecration God cleanses our hearts from all sin and fills us with His Holy Spirit. Although we call it entire sanctification, it is wrong to conclude that God is finished with us. He has only begun what can best be described as a lifetime of progressive sanctification. During our lifetimes we should always be growing spiritually, becoming more mature, and becoming more like Jesus. Final sanctification will occur when we see Jesus face-to-face. When we see Him, in that moment, we will become like Him.

Understanding God's role in entire sanctification helps us understand our need for the Holy

Spirit's presence in our hearts and minds. You may be asking yourself, *Is it possible for God to cleanse me from all sin and enable me (for any extended period of time) to live above known, willful, and conscious sin?*

The church at Corinth is an example of the need in every born-again believer's life for a work of grace that more deeply and thoroughly cleanses his or her heart. The Christians who made up the church at Corinth and to whom Paul wrote his letter had paid an enormously high price for deciding to follow Jesus. Paul addressed the conflict that arose within the new church mission in his letter.

Are you surprised that there was conflict in the Corinth church? The truth is, then and now, whenever and wherever you deal with people—even though they are saved and following Christ—there will eventually be issues that surface that cause discord and conflict. Conflict occurs at every level—the local church, denominational headquarters, or even on the mission field. Paul recognized this in the church at Corinth as he witnessed the rise of envy and strife in the midst of the congregation.

How did this happen among saved people who had decided to follow Jesus? These were Christians who responded enthusiastically to the call of God. Many of them had made great sacrifices to ally themselves with this radical upstart of a church.

The simple explanation is that there still exists in the heart of the born-again believer a tendency toward sin. This is a by-product of human nature, and it is in constant conflict with the Spirit of Christ that lives within the believer. A spiritual, internal warfare is taking place.

What can God do about it? Has He made provision for this condition, or is it something we just have to learn to live with? When Jesus gave himself over to the Cross, He made provision for a deeper cleansing of our souls from the sin that remains after we turn to Him and repent. Jesus went to the Cross to sanctify us with His blood.

I was privileged to hold a series of revival meetings at Asbury College. Many of the seminary students participated in the services. One night at the close of the service two seminarians, a young man and a young lady, came to the platform to speak to me. The young man said, "I came on Monday morning to listen to you preach, and you preached a sermon on sanctification. I had never heard a sermon on that subject before. I come from a Bible-believing, evangelical church, and we have revival meetings, yet I had never heard of this. As you were preaching, I decided what you were saying was heresy and wrote you off. I decided to come back and have been here every morning and evening, and you have been preaching this stuff all week!" He continued, "I've been going from the library to my Bible trying to prove you wrong. After last night's service I couldn't stand it any longer. I went back to my apartment, locked the door, and got down on my knees with my Bible in front of me and prayed, 'Lord, if this is truth, if this is biblical, if this is Your plan and Your will for Your people and for Your Church, I want You to show it to me in Your Word. Lord, when You show it to me in Your Word I will not get off of my knees until You have met this need in my heart and life. But, Lord, if it isn't truth, if it isn't real, I want You to show it to me so that I won't be bothered by this stuff anymore.'"

He said, "I prayed and I read until the early hours of the morning, until I was totally exhausted—so much so that I just became quiet for a little time. Then it happened. When I got quiet, the Holy Spirit drew my attention back to a revival meeting held at my home church three years ago. Although I was young, I was considered to be one of the spiritual leaders of the church. Following the last meeting on a Sunday night, everyone who had attended left the church in high spirits, blessed by the service and the meeting's successful conclusion. I was so depressed because unknown to anyone there was an area of my life that defeated me repeatedly. I went home and threw myself across my bed and in prayer told the Lord I would do anything He wanted me to do, go anywhere He wanted me to go, and be anything He wanted me to be if He would only give me victory over this area of my life."

The young man's demeanor began to change as I listened to him continue. "That night God met a need in my heart, and I've never been the same since that moment. The temptation has returned, but by His grace, I have been able to resist it and remain victorious. Because of the prayer meeting I had with God that night, I answered His call for me to preach and to prepare by enrolling here at the seminary.

"Last night when I got quiet before the Lord, I felt the Holy Spirit telling me that He had done for me that night what you have been preaching about all week!"

He then asked me, "Do you believe that is possible? Could God have sanctified me that night, even though I had never heard a sermon on the subject?"

I told him, "I would never question a testimony like yours! When you make that kind of commitment to God and yield all that you did, there isn't any question in my mind that is exactly what God did for you that night."

Then the young lady looked at me. She had

heard the message of heart holiness and entire sanctification her entire life. She explained that she wanted everything God had planned for her and to be completely consecrated as His servant. But there was a question haunting her life. "Do you really believe that it's possible to live above known, willful, conscious sin for any extended period of time?"

I looked at her and replied, "Let me ask you a question. Do you think that there is something so inadequate in the work of Jesus upon the Cross that He cannot solve your sin problem and my sin problem and help us to live victoriously?"

She answered, "I wouldn't want to settle for anything less!"

I said, "That's great! You got the right answer to question number one; now here is question number two. Do you think that if God could cleanse a person's heart and fill that person with His Holy Spirit He could empower that person to live above known, willful sin for five minutes?"

She looked up at me and said, "Well, yes, I believe God could keep me victorious over sin for five minutes."

I asked her, "What about five hours?" and she said, "Oh, yes!"

"God is getting bigger all of the time, isn't He?" I said, "What an awesome God we serve. Do you think that if the time were stretched to five days, with all the possibility for the devil to tempt and cajole you, that God could empower you to live above sinning?"

She thought for a moment and all of a sudden I saw tears well up in her eyes, and she said, "You know, I've never thought of it that way before. Yes, I believe in that kind of God. Right now in this moment I claim Him not only as my Savior but also as my Sanctifier, and I claim His sanctifying grace." In that very moment the presence of the Spirit of God was overwhelming.

I reminded both of them, "You will never be so holy but what you will still be human. In your humanity, you will be tempted. As a free moral agent with freedom of choice there is always the possibility that in a moment of weakness you might yield to that temptation and commit sin. The possibility will always exist. Sinless perfection is not biblical. We do not believe it's impossible to sin this side of heaven, but what we do believe is that it's possible to not sin by the grace of God. We can always make the decision to say no to the temptations and to say yes to God."

I also reminded them that John said, "My dear children, I write this to you so that you will not sin. But if anybody does sin, we have one who speaks to the Father in our defense—Jesus Christ, the Righteous One" (1 John 2:1) so that when we do sin, if we will call on His name and seek His forgiveness, God for Jesus' sake will blot out that transgression and you can be spiritually renewed and restored. It is this hope that helps us learn from our experiences and live a consistent, successful, holy life that will honor and glorify God.

George Mueller, who was used by God to help many orphans, was sanctified four years after he made a decision to follow Christ. He testified, "When I was sanctified, I was instantly delivered from the love of money and the love of place, and the love for worldly pleasure." Sixty years later Mueller, while on his deathbed, said, "I have walked with God for sixty years in unbroken fellowship." It may be tempting to say, "What a man!" but more accurately we could say, "What a God!" Who but God could reach down into this sin-cursed, fallen world and pick up a poor, lost, guilty, hell-deserving sinner and so transform his life! How extraordinary that he could live in our world, fully human, for even five minutes without sinning!

I wish my testimony was as succinct as Mueller's. I wish that from the night I settled the issues that separated me from such a walk with God while I was still a freshman on the campus of Circleville Bible College that there had never been a moment of broken fellowship with Him. I believe in those possibilities under God's grace. But I have to be honest and say there have been times along my spiritual journey when I have fallen on my face before God with a broken heart. I have openly wept before Him and cried out, "O God, I've messed things up and sinned, and I'm sorry. Please blot out my transgression."

I didn't deserve it, but every time He instantly blotted out that transgression, and there was a restoration of fellowship. There have been times I have had to ask my friends and family to forgive me, as well as people with whom I have worked. In every instance, God graciously forgave me. His grace was sufficient, and by the blood of Jesus Christ there was beautiful restoration.

A young lady I know participated in a mission trip to South America and felt her heart broken by the need of the people to whom she ministered. Upon her return to the United States, she explained that she had prayed and accepted a call by God to become a career missionary and wanted to meet with our mission board. We began our dialogue and the interview process with her. Since she was heavily involved in a local holiness church, we were puzzled to see a blank look cross her face when we asked her to tell us about her experience of entire sanctification. Finally, she summoned the courage to respond, "What is that? I've never heard of it."

It was my privilege to give her a brief explanation of the term, and then I said to her, "I'm going to support you with all the information I can offer you—tapes and books—and I want you to take them with you and digest them."

One night she walked into a service where I was preaching, and she was the first person to respond to the invitation to the altar to seek a pure heart by means of sanctification. I will never forget what she said to me several weeks later: "I do not understand why every Christian wouldn't want this deeper work of grace! For the first time in my life, I have hope that when I get up in the morning that it is going to be possible by God's grace to live a victorious, consistent life. I was born and raised in a parsonage and attended Christian colleges, but I have never felt such hope and peace. I'm going to ask my pastor why he never preaches on this subject. I think everybody ought to know about it."

As a follower of Christ, have you accepted all that God has for you? Have you experienced this deeper cleansing in your spiritual walk with God? It is a liberating work of grace that will free you from self-centeredness and selfish ambition. If you have not accepted it, it is exactly what you need and exactly what God wants you to experience. It is a gift that God freely gives to you. Jesus suffered the disdain and the humility of the Cross so that you might enjoy the fellowship of the Holy Spirit by the sacrifice of His own blood. Have you allowed God to do what He desires in every part of your life?

7

The Process of Sanctification

And so Jesus also suffered outside the city gate to make the people holy through his own blood (Heb. 13:12).

In our zeal to promote scriptural holiness we have sometimes made the doctrine of entire sanctification seem as though it cured every shortcoming, weakness, and human limitation. The fact is, even those who are holy are still human. In 2 Cor. 4:7, Paul says, "We have this treasure in jars of clay to show that this all-surpassing power is from God and not from us." "Jars of clay," or "earthen vessels" as referred to in the King James Version, is talking about our humanness.

Entire sanctification is designed by God to deal with the human will and sinful bent, but it does not instantly "cure" us of human imperfections. When entire sanctification takes place and our hearts are cleansed and made pure, no sin remains to pollute or contaminate the heart. The heart is "made perfect in love" (1 John 4:18, KJV). Being "made perfect in love" means that the heart of the believer is no longer divided in its affections and leaning toward sin but, instead, the heart is now set on doing what is right. Jesus Christ sits on the throne of the sanctified believer's heart and becomes the supreme love of that person's life.

You can have a heart that is perfect in God's sight—pure and clean. You can have Jesus Christ as the center of your affections. But you will still be an imperfect human being. Sanctification does not perfect your intellect or your *judgment.* Sanctification will not perfect your *performance.* What will become perfect is your love for God and the purity of your intent. Your motives will be purified and cleansed.

It is important to know what we cannot expect when we experience sanctification. Entire sanctification will not give us physical health. Sometimes we are quick to judge one another's spiritual state by grouchy, irritable behavior when all that's really needed is a good night's sleep. We are earthen—made from the dust of the earth. Because of that, even in the sanctified life, there remains a need for repentance when we behave badly.

I knew a holiness preacher once who told me he

never apologized to his children because they might lose confidence in his sanctification. I feel certain that they had already lost confidence in him. It would have been far better if he had asked his children for forgiveness when he behaved badly. Our God is merciful, patient, and quick to forgive.

Entire sanctification is not going to instantly give you strong emotional strength. If perfect patience and emotional poise could be guaranteed, our churches would be packed. Although sanctification cleanses the heart from all sin, patience develops during the process of living a holy life. Don't make the mistake of thinking that because you lack patience you are not sanctified. Just repent of your earthen frailty and ask God to forgive you and help you in that area. Then continue in your spiritual walk.

Entire sanctification does not guarantee that you will never be tempted. Even Jesus was tempted. Adam and Eve were tempted. Sanctified persons will be tempted. You will be tempted in ways that are contrary to the will of God. Being tempted is not a sin, nor is the urge to do wrong a sin. It is just temptation. Not until we consent with our hearts and minds, hands or mouths, does temptation become sin. We must constantly choose between right and wrong. Through the power of the Spirit we can say no when we're tempted.

Entire sanctification does not cleanse us from the learned and acquired habits we have cultivated in our lives. Peter is a good example. He demonstrated great prejudice toward the Gentile church after he was baptized with the Holy Spirit on the Day of Pentecost. The root of his sin problem had been eradicated, but the things he had learned over the years were not instantly dealt with when he was filled with God's Spirit. God later worked dramatically to reveal to Peter through a vision that there was prejudice in his heart (see Acts 19:9-48).

Sanctification is both immediate and progressive. The immediate cleansing of our heart's sin is the beginning of our progressive sanctification as God deals with those things we have picked up in our lives that hinder us from being effective witnesses to His Spirit's work. Every sanctified person will have "blind spots" in his or her relationship with God. Entire sanctification puts us on the road to becoming more like Jesus every day. He will give you insight within your spirit as His Spirit shows you the areas that need modification to better reflect holiness.

I have a friend who was an alcoholic before he was saved. He said, "From the moment I was saved I've never had any desire to taste alcohol again. There has never been a moment when I've been tempted to go back to alcohol." I thank God for that testimony and rejoice in my friend's wonderful deliverance. However, I have known others who, even after being sanctified, have battled addictions on every front. They asked God to deliver them but continued to struggle with what they knew were sinful habits. They are a part of who we are spiritually, psychologically, and physically. One thing is certain, though. When God convicts you of your need for deliverance from some sin in your life, He stands ready and able to deliver you. Only as we surrender these habits to God can we find victory and freedom from them!

Entire sanctification will not cleanse your subconscious. It cleanses your heart from sin but does not remove the sinful experiences that may affect you after you are filled with the Holy Spirit. You will probably remember the things you were involved in before accepting Christ as your Savior and Sanctifier.

A retired pastor came to me and said, "My wife is in the nursing home and she doesn't remember me anymore. I go to see her every day, and I make certain she eats at least one good meal. It is getting harder and harder for me to go. She no longer remembers me and now she curses and fills the air with profanity. We've been married for more than 60 years, and in that whole time I have never heard a derogatory word come out of her mouth. Is it possible that in her weakened condition she has become demon possessed?"

I replied, "Absolutely not! There is no way a child of God can become possessed by a demon unless he or she opens the door to them. Her problem stems from having heard those words at some time in her past, and they are lodged in her memory. Now, for some reason, they are coming out of her lips, but not of her volition. If she were in control of her faculties, she would never utter those words; they do not represent the condition of her soul. God knows her heart and judges her based on her heart. She is not accountable for the things she is not aware of doing and saying."

There is so much that entire sanctification does for us, but experiencing it does not mean you have "arrived" and that there is nothing left for the Holy Spirit to teach you. Entire sanctification is just the beginning of all that God has for you as He helps you grow in the grace He provides for each new circumstance.

There came a time in my life that the beauty, holiness, and gentleness of Jesus captured me—I wanted to be just like Him. I would try—and fail. I would try again—and fail again. Then one day I realized that I could have Him on the throne of my heart and that He could live in me. Then, by His power, purity, and precious love flowing through me, I would be like Him. He isn't finished with me yet. He helps me daily to conform more and more to His likeness. He is in control and free to do whatever He wills in my heart.

Is Jesus in control of your life? Does He have the freedom to do His perfect work in you? Let the Holy Spirit fill your life every day and empower you to be like Jesus Christ.

8

The Disposition of the Sanctified

The population of Markle, Indiana, is 1,140. There's a large sign on the outskirts of town that reads, "The home of 1,136 happy people and four old grouches." Every time I pass through that town, I wonder, "Who are the four grouches, and do they know who they are?" Then I think, "This would be a pretty good town to live in if there are only four grouches living in it." You may have more grouches than that living in your *house.*

"If you have any encouragement from being united with Christ, if any comfort from his love, if any fellowship with the Spirit, if any tenderness and compassion, then make my joy complete by being like-minded, having the same love, being one in spirit and purpose. Do nothing out of selfish ambition or vain conceit, but in humility consider others better than yourselves. Each of you should look not only to your own interests, but also to the interests of others. Your attitude should be the same as that of Christ Jesus: Who, being in very nature God, did not consider equality with God something to be grasped, but made himself nothing, taking the very nature of a servant, being made in human likeness. And being found in appearance as a man, he humbled himself and became obedient to death—even death on a cross! Therefore God exalted him to the highest place and gave him the name that is above every name, that at the name of Jesus every knee should bow, in heaven and on earth and under the earth, and every tongue confess that Jesus Christ is Lord, to the glory of God the Father" (Phil. 2:1-11).

Notice especially verse 5, "Your attitude [or your disposition] should be the same as that of Christ Jesus," or as the King James Version reads, "Let this mind be in you, which was also in Christ Jesus."

E. Stanley Jones was one of the greatest missionaries to India. His influence was felt worldwide in the Christian community. On one occasion he asked the Hindu leader Gandhi what he could do to increase the effectiveness of Christianity in India. Gandhi's response was, "All Christians, including the missionaries, must begin to live more like Jesus Christ." With that statement, Gandhi identified what I believe is one of the greatest needs in the Christian church: we should be more Christlike.

As a young man Gandhi studied Christianity and the teachings of Jesus, even to the point of considering becoming a Christian. At that time, living in South Africa when racism was rampant and apartheid was not a widely known word, he was repeatedly turned away from Christian churches because of the color of his skin. Ultimately he rejected Christianity, saying that he was very attracted to Christ and His teachings but that he rarely met a Christian who was very much like Him. What a tragic indictment against the Body of Christ!

Paul reminds us that we are also to be vessels for the mind of Christ. The mind is an interesting thing. You cannot see your mind or x-ray it. You cannot take a biopsy of it, yet it is real. It controls your attitudes and actions. You can see and x-ray your brain, but not the mind that controls it. We cannot have the brain of Christ, but we can have the mind of Christ, or rather His disposition.

It seems to me that the world should see Christ in us. Simplistic, you may say, but is it really? Have you asked yourself what others see when they look at you? The world is hungry to see Jesus. Many revere Muhammad, Buddha, and Allah as gods, but what is it about Jesus that makes a real difference in a person's life? These same people who are watching Christians understand that we go to church, sometimes twice on Sunday, sometimes in the middle of the week. They may know that Christians give money to the church in the form of a tithe and participate in charitable causes. But what they really want to know is what difference does Jesus make in your life when your world is crumbling and your heart is broken? What does He do for you when your spouse leaves and your children disappoint you or when you are fired from your job or the factory closes and you don't know how you are going to pay the bills at home? Can Jesus do anything then?

Paul tells us it is the intention of God that we be conformed to the likeness of Christ, His Son. If we are to be conformed to that image, people should see Christ in your attitudes, your actions, your reactions, and your responses.

If we have the *disposition* of Christ, it will make a difference in the very atmosphere of our lives. The atmosphere that characterized Jesus' life can be summed up in one word—peace. He was and remains the Prince of Peace. It is His will that we live in peace (see Isa. 9:6). In this passage Paul piles one phrase upon the other, emphasizing that the atmosphere surrounding the life of a Spirit-filled, sanctified believer should be one of peace. "Being like-minded, having the same love, being one in spirit and purpose." Be of one mind. Discord, division, and factions in the church and in the life of the believer grieve the Holy Spirit. If we as a church are of one accord and filled with the Holy Spirit, then we ought to get along! To testify that you have the mind of Christ yet can't get along with people in your own church is a contradiction and reproach to the cause of the gospel.

I believe that our relationships with one another are good indications of the relationship each of us has with the Lord Jesus Christ. This is not to say that saints cannot have strong, differing opinions.

On one occasion a pastor said to me, "I told the board last month that if they were prayed up, paid up, and truly sanctified and in the center of God's will that we would never have a disagreement in a board meeting."

I said, "You didn't really tell them that, did you?"

He replied, "Yes, I did!"

"You don't believe that, do you?" I asked, even more shocked.

And he said, "Yes, I do. Don't you?"

I finished, saying, "No, I really don't."

All of us come from different backgrounds, experiences, and degrees of knowledge. Some of us have a greater ability to take facts, assimilate them, and come to logical conclusions. These are not abilities that are dependent upon your sanctification, rather they are abilities that we bring to God, and He uses each in accordance with what we know and understand. Regardless of your spiritual integrity and maturity, the fact remains that sanctified believers of God will always see some things differently. You will always encounter differences in opinions and ideas. What the mind of Christ enables us to do is to disagree amicably. Even in times of strong dissension we can disagree with kindness, courtesy, and respect for each other.

How do you feel about your attitude toward those with whom you disagree? How can bitterness, malice, jealousy, a vengeful and unforgiving spirit, or a "holier than thou" attitude in any way be compatible with the mind of Christ? Cliques, divisions, and factions are incompatible with the indwelling of the Holy Spirit, and Satan uses every opportunity he is given to sow the seed of strife.

Peace. Jesus said, "Blessed are the peacemakers, for they will be called sons of God" (Matt. 5:9). The world is looking for solid evidence that people are completely sold out to God, filled with His Spirit, and living a holy life. The pursuit of peace in your life cannot be something you seek only for yourself. It must also be something that is on clear display for your neighbor, coworker, and family to see.

There are some mountains worth dying upon and some things worth fighting for. Choose your battles wisely and carefully to make certain they are battles of great principle and truth. Our battles must be marked by the presence and spirit of Christ, and we must understand who we represent and the implications that has for bringing His peace into the midst of our journeys.

I was holding a revival meeting, and the first night of the revival I arrived late. The service had already begun, so while the congregation was singing, I ran up to the platform and sat down. Within five minutes I was on my feet preaching. We were in a beautiful new church building that was to be dedicated the following Sunday. I commented about what a beautiful church they had built and continued my sermon. Somehow, purely unintentionally, in the middle of my message I began to meddle. I hit them like a steamroller with, "Sometimes when we get into these building programs we will fuss, fight, and quarrel over such trivial and insignificant things. Over matters of personal prejudice we get so passionate that we allow the devil a great opportunity to split and divide us. We will fuss over the color of the carpet and whether or not to pad the pews. We argue over whether or not to bring the old bell from the old church and hang it in the new church and whether or not to take those pictures from the old church and hang them in the new one."

At that point I knew I had struck a nerve, because the people went ballistic. When I finished the message the pastor ran onto the platform and began, "Folks, I want you to know I didn't tell this evangelist anything. I never told him about our last business meeting when we had that big fuss over whether or not we were going to bring the bell from the old church and put it into this one. I never said a word to him about how we fought over those pictures and where we would hang them. But if the shoe fits, you're going to have to wear it, because I haven't said a word to him!"

By that point it was my turn to laugh! The pastor asked me how I knew. I told him I didn't know but that I'd been in some building programs before as well, and I know how the devil takes advantage of human nature to use those things to break up a good church.

As believers, we should each seek understanding and peace with those who oppose us. Peace is one of the evidences of a genuine work of grace in the life of a believer. Are you a peacemaker?

If you take the disposition of Christ upon yourself, it will make a difference in your attitude toward life. I believe that a powerful characteristic of the life of Christ is His complete unselfishness. He surrendered himself that you and I might be redeemed. This theological view is called the "great kenosis" or the "self-emptying" of Christ (see Phil. 2:7). "Who, being in very nature God, did not consider equality with God something to be grasped, but made himself nothing, taking the very nature of a servant, being in human likeness. And being found in appearance as a man, he humbled himself and became obedient to death—even death on a cross!" (Phil. 2:6-8).

Status was not important to Christ. He voluntarily gave up His glory to become a man—but not just a man; He also became a servant, although no ordinary servant. Jesus gave up His life to death and the grave by way of the Cross. "Greater love has no one than this, that he lay down his life for his friends" (John 15:13). He was totally unselfish and completely submissive to His Father.

What a challenge this is to Christians today who are constantly bombarded with the message that our own wants and needs and rights should come first. Our society has defiled what God created and glorifies whatever is the fad of the moment. Humans are, by nature, self-centered. You do not have to teach children to be selfish. In fact, you have to work diligently to teach them unselfishness. To enjoy God's grace, the Christian must empty himself or herself and surrender to God's plan for his or her life.

To be submissive, self-sacrificing, and humble is not popular—or easy. But to be like Jesus it is necessary. Jesus did not retaliate to man's injustices or strike back when they spit upon Him. He turned the other cheek and went the second mile. He taught us to forgive 70 times 7. These traits are indicative of the strong character God wants to instill within you.

If we have the disposition of Christ, it will make a difference in the actions of our lives. Every activity in which Jesus was involved was meant to honor God and bless humankind. If you have the mind of Christ, the passion of your heart will be to glorify God in your witness and to bless those around you. No longer will you ask, "Is it right or wrong?" Instead the questions are deeper. "Will it glorify God," and "How will it influence my witness for Jesus?"

When you fall in love with Jesus and He becomes the Lord of your life, your influence becomes precious. Friends and family will be looking for the Christ you claim to possess. Some activities that you could take part in will not destroy your relationship with Jesus but could destroy your *influence* for Him, so think carefully before taking action.

A missionary who served for many years was on a flight in Eastern Europe. The flight attendant brought the missionary his meal accompanied by the small bottle of wine that accompanies all meals served on flights in that area of the world.

He thought to himself, "I could probably drink the wine and it wouldn't cause me to lose fellowship with Jesus. I am in the middle of nowhere, and nobody on this plane knows who I am," but he had no intention of drinking it. When the flight attendant picked up his tray, the man across the aisle leaned over and said, "Excuse me sir, aren't you ———?" using the missionary's name. In great surprise the missionary said, "Yes." The gentleman said, "I thought that was who you were. You preached in my church just a couple of weeks ago, and I was sure that was you." My friend breathed a prayer and said, "Thank You, Lord, for helping me guard my actions."

The world is watching you and me. They *want* to see that Jesus makes a difference. They *want* to see differences in our activities and our behavior. There are some things you might be able to do that you don't do because it could be a stumbling block to a new Christian. We also must be aware of the bigger questions, "Does it glorify God," and "How does it affect my witness?" No longer do we ask "What's in it for me?" Instead we offer ourselves to Him with, "Here I am Lord, send me."

My father told me a story about a businessman who, before he went to work one Monday morning, spent a few extra minutes in prayer asking God to help him be more like Jesus in his relationships, conversations, actions, attitudes, and reactions. He walked to the train station as usual where people gathered to ride the train into the city to work. As always, the boarding platform was jammed with commuters. When the train pulled into the station, everybody began pushing and shoving to get into it. As he tried to push his way onto the train, he bumped into a little boy who carried a brown paper sack, and the man accidentally knocked the sack out of the little boy's hand. It fell to the platform and broke open, spilling its contents onto the concrete. Spread everywhere were hundreds of pieces of a jigsaw puzzle. His first thought was, "If I don't get on this train, I'll be late for work." Immediately he prayed, "Lord, help me to be more like Jesus." He went back and helped that little boy pick up every piece of the puzzle they could find and put them all back into the sack. As he put the last piece back in the sack, the little boy looked up at the businessman and asked, "Mister, are you Jesus?"

Has anyone mistaken you for Jesus lately? Or are you more likely to be mistaken for one of the four grouches in Markle, Indiana, population 1,140?

9

The Highway of Holiness

The desert and the parched land will be glad; the wilderness will rejoice and blossom. Like the crocus, it will burst into bloom; it will rejoice greatly and shout for joy. The glory of Lebanon will be given to it, the splendor of Carmel and Sharon; they will see the glory of the LORD, the splendor of our God. Strengthen the feeble hands, steady the knees that give way; say to those with fearful hearts, 'Be strong, do not fear; your God will come, he will come with vengeance; with divine retribution he will come to save you.' Then will the eyes of the blind be opened and the ears of the deaf unstopped. Then will the lame leap like a deer, and the mute tongue shout for joy. Water will gush forth in the wilderness and streams in the desert. The burning sand will become a pool, the thirsty ground bubbling springs. In the haunts where jack-

als once lay, grass and reeds and papyrus will grow. And a highway will be there; it will be called the Way of Holiness. The unclean will not journey on it; it will be for those who walk in that Way; wicked fools will not go about on it. No lion will be there, nor will any ferocious beast get up on it; they will not be found there. But only the redeemed will walk there, and the ransomed of the LORD *will return. They will enter Zion with singing; everlasting joy will crown their heads. Gladness and joy will overtake them, and sorrow and sighing will flee away* (Isa. 35:1-10).

Most likely, you have traveled many highways during your life. As I think about the roads I have traveled, I believe the most beautiful is Route One on the western coast of the United States. On one side spans the Pacific Ocean and on the other are mountain ranges named Shasta, the Cascades, the Olympics and Willapas, and the Sierra Madre.

The most breathtaking *road* I have traveled isn't a highway at all. It is more of a combination of a paved street and gravel road, and it is located on the island of Barbados. My trip started in the town of Bridgetown and wound along the western coast for about five miles. Eventually there is a sharp turn from the turquoise waters of the Caribbean to the interior of the island, immediately aimed skyward. As the road climbs Mount Hillaby there are potholes to dodge, children, and the black-bellied sheep Barbados is known for. The road becomes enclosed by the semitropical foliage, beautiful flowers, and green monkeys. Then, all at once, the road reaches the mountain's peak and one beholds the expanse of the eastern side of the island with the seemingly endless horizon of the Atlantic Ocean. The site is so magnificent that for a moment it seems everything stops. It's absolutely breathtaking.

One of the most *congested* highways I have ever traveled is the 405 in Los Angeles, with its tributaries likened more to a bowl of spaghetti than an interstate system. Sometimes all 16 lanes of traffic move at an almost blinding speed, and then as fast as they are moving all lanes can come to a complete halt.

The *speediest* of all highways I have ever traveled is the Autobahn in Germany. No speed limits. Even as I cruised along at 70 or 80 miles per hour, vehicles passed me like I was parked.

The most *frightening* highway I have ever traveled is in Kenya in the area of West Pokot. It took two and one-half hours to move along the last 10 kilometers that wind up a steep mountain. There are no guardrails or protection of any kind, and the edge of the road dramatically drops straight down —way down. A glance over the edge squelches even the slightest temptation to be reckless. Numerous cars that failed to stay on the road are strewn along the side of the cliff and on precipice after precipice. It is a virtual vertical vehicle graveyard. There is no way to retrieve the cars, so they hang there, a spooky reminder of what could happen. The road is filled with hairpin curves, which is the reason I always carry a camera when I'm there. Usually I never carry a camera because I don't want to look like a tourist. But when traveling that highway I always carry a camera, whether or not it has film in it. That way when we get to one of those hairpin curves it gives me reason to ask the driver to let me out of the car. I simply say, "I've got to get a picture of this; the people back home will never believe it!" So I get out and pretend I'm taking a picture and then walk around the curve.

The *longest* road I've ever been on is the last 50 miles from anywhere to home. It is particularly true when the weather is bad, I'm dead tired, I've been gone for a long time, and it is two o'clock in the morning. Under those conditions it seems as though that last 50 miles last forever.

The most *important* highway that you or I will ever travel is not manmade but rather God-made. It is called the highway of holiness. If you are not traveling this highway, you should consider getting on it immediately, because its destination is a place called heaven. It is the only highway that leads to heaven and into eternal life.

The first thing I want you to notice about this highway is that it is excellent. The Hebrew word that is used here for "highway" carries the connotation of being a constructed way. It is a lifted-up, leveled, and prepared roadway. It is described in stark contrast to a simple path that might wind through the grass or the sand. It implies that it is a carefully constructed road upon which royalty is meant to travel. It implies that the valleys have been raised, the mountains leveled, and the stones and potholes removed. It is an excellent highway.

This highway reminds me of what they do in Kenya when the country's president is coming into a particular area. They get out the graders and dozers and smooth the way in anticipation of his arrival. In so doing, the road is smoothed, the potholes are filled, and the errant pavement or stones are pushed to the side. When the president travels the road it is smooth, and he, along with his entourage, moves into and out of the area quickly. God has prepared an excellent highway for His family. It is imperative that you do not miss entering this highway of holiness. You will never find another road more satisfying or fulfilling.

While I was in college my parents pastored a

church in Endicott, New York. The school I attended was in Ohio, so several times a year I drove from Ohio to New York and back again. In those days the only good route to New York was straight through Pittsburgh. We didn't have the superhighways we have today. Instead, we traveled from one stoplight to the next in bumper-to-bumper traffic. During the summer months it felt as though the smoke from the factories and refineries could suffocate a person. It was a miserable part of the journey. Now there are superhighways raised above the city streets that take one right over the city without dealing with stoplights. Even though there are streets below with traffic that is still bumper-to-bumper, traffic light after traffic light, the cars on the new highway cruise along with no obstructions or hindrances.

The excellent highway of holiness follows this same metaphor. It does not curve and deviate into the muck and mire or filth and stench of the world. It is so clear and straight that even the simple-minded can find it. It is a secure and safe way, undisturbed by wild beasts and never traveled by wicked fools. Of course, trials and temptation are as numerous as exit ramps because the devil is looking for ways to lure people off of this road, but the highway of holiness is still there and always has available traveling space.

In contrast, the road to financial success is booby-trapped with the temptation to covet and be greedy. The road to fame is trapped with vanity, self-centeredness, and compromise. The road to professional success is mined with complacency, but the path to holiness leads only to more holiness on this excellent way.

It is also an encouraging way. The prophet tells us, "Strengthen the feeble hands, steady the knees that give way; say to those with fearful hearts, 'Be strong, do not fear; your God will come, he will come with vengeance; with divine retribution he will come to save you" (Isa. 35:3-4). On the highway of holiness there will always be the strong and the healthy, the weak and the feeble. If you are traveling on this road, you have the responsibility to reach out to those who are weak, feeble, hurting, or in trouble.

My friend Bill is now a pastor, but when he was in high school he was on the boys' cross-country team. Cross-country running is not always the most popular sport, and it takes a great deal of discipline and passion. It is highly individualistic, often with no one along the way to cheer you. Bill's coach knew very little about the technical aspects of running, but he had great insight into human nature. Every time there was a cross-country meet, he recruited girls from the school to position themselves in small groups along the track, and as the runners went past, the girls were supposed to cheer them along. Also, Bill's coach allowed anyone on the team who had a girlfriend to position that special friend at the finish line. The entire time Bill was on this team they never lost a competition, and not one person ever dropped out of a race.

The highway of holiness is filled with travelers who are encouragers, and best of all God is cheering us along. He will save us and help us to overcome all obstacles we encounter. God is with us, He is for us, and He is in us.

The highway of holiness is also an exclusive way. Isa. 35:8-9 tells us, "The unclean will not journey on it; . . . wicked fools will not go about on it. No lion will be there, nor will any ferocious beast get up on it; . . . but only the redeemed will walk there." That makes it exclusive as to who may travel upon it, but it is also inclusive in that every person is *invited* to travel on it. The rich and the poor, the weak and the strong, the educated and the uneducated, and people from every culture, race, and continent are included in the invitation.

You cannot travel the highway of holiness with willful sin in your life. The people who travel this road have been slaves to the sin in their lives but now are servants of righteousness. They were in bondage to evil passions but now are set free from sin. They used to fulfill their own desires, but now they live for God and seek to glorify Him.

How do you get on this highway? The entry ramp to the highway of holiness begins at the point you repent of your sins and trust Jesus Christ as your Savior. Many people believe that this is the end to all God has for us, but actually conversion is only the beginning. God designed it so that our conversion is followed by sanctification and a lifetime of walking with God, coming to know Him better, and growing in grace. God is primarily interested in forgiving us of our sins, but He is also interested in transforming our character and shaping us more into the image of Jesus Christ. This exclusive road is one leading to victory, not despair and defeat.

In the 1972 Olympic games the United States swim team swept the competition and won the bronze, silver, and gold medals in most competitions, setting record after record in many events. Before the swim events began, the television cameras and sports personalities gave brief glances into the lives of the U.S. swimmers. They looked strange to me. The male swimmers had shaved all the hair from their bodies, from their legs to their heads. This was before the "bald look" was popular. One evening they interviewed one of the swimmers and asked him why they had shaved as they had. His reply went something like this: "We are here to bring the gold, the silver, and the bronze back to America. The best swimmers in the world are here. Races will be won by fractions of seconds, and world records will fall as new ones are set. We are here to excel. We are here to do the best we are capable of doing. We have shaved all the hair from our bodies so there will be much less resistance in the water. We want to swim the fastest races possible."

I sat in my living room and chuckled, thinking, "What a bunch of fanatics." But when those Olympic games were over and Mark Spitz and his teammates had rewritten the record times for swimming, I admired their dedication to excellence. They became heroes because they had an objective and they wanted nothing to stand in their way.

If we're going to live for Jesus, we should strive for excellence in every aspect of our lives. We should endeavor to be more like Him and allow nothing to stand in our way to achieve that goal. We must "throw off everything that hinders and the sin that so easily entangles" (Heb. 12:1), making certain we are running a good race.

The highway of holiness is also an exuberant way. In verse 10 of Isa. 35, "The ransomed of the Lord will return. They will enter Zion with singing; everlasting joy will crown their heads. Gladness and joy will overtake them, and sorrow and sighing will flee away." Have you ever felt like someone was following you? Did it ever occur to you that it might be gladness and joy? That is what God is saying through the prophet Isaiah. The highway of holiness leads from bondage to freedom, from sin to holiness, and from selfishness to service. The people who travel this road are exuberant because they are ransomed and redeemed. They were in bondage and slaves to sin, but now they are delivered. They are on the road to eternal life with heaven as their destination.

We are on a march to Zion. We are looking forward to seeing and entering the city of God. It is a place of absolute security where there are neither trials nor temptation. As we travel this road we should be filled with the joy and excitement of knowing we are on a march to a city where there are no infirmities, sorrow, suffering, or tears. The closer we get, the greater our excitement will be.

As Christ created it, our Church is a singing church—joyful and triumphant. We have been set free, and the joy we may experience here is just a small portion of the exuberance we will experience there!

Ed is a pastor who resides in Colorado Springs, and he was looking for an adequate illustration of the Church. He visited the Air Force Academy and watched the airmen march with precision and grace. He thought, "Maybe that's a good example. After all, 'Onward Christian soldiers, marching as to war.'" He went to a football game and watched the teams with players of different sizes and shapes, each with a role to fill. They were pulling together as a team to be victorious. Again he thought, "Maybe that's a good example. Every person has a role to fill, all working together to be victorious." Then one day the Special Olympics came to town, and he went to watch them compete. To prepare for the 40-yard dash a group of children queued up at the starting line. They took off running at the crack of the start pistol. Running as fast as they were able, suddenly one of the little fellows stumbled and fell, then sat on the track and cried. When the other runners heard him crying, they stopped running and turned to see what had happened. Together they ran back to the little boy, picked him up, and brushed him off. He had a scrape on his forehead, and one little girl leaned over and kissed it saying, "Now it's all better and it won't hurt anymore." Then they all joined hands and finished the rest of the race hand in hand, crossing the finish line together. Ed decided, "Now there is the Church."

There are times on the highway when a fellow

brother or sister stumbles. He or she may get discouraged, downtrodden, and depressed. We must be sensitive to the needs of those around us, and as we hear their cries and see them fall we must run to them and pick them up. We must take them by their hands and help them in the journey until they are able to walk on their own again, finishing our "race" together.

Ike Skelton's big dream as a high school student was to run the mile for his school's track team. He trained hard year round. He went to bed early and rose early to train. He ate healthy and stayed away from junk food. He disciplined himself, working harder than every other athlete in that school. When he was a freshman, he managed to make the team but never was allowed the opportunity to run for them in competition. The same thing happened his sophomore year, his junior year, and his senior year. Near the end of the season Ike's coach came to him and said, "Ike, this Saturday you are going to run the mile." His coach knew how long and hard he had prepared for the event. When word spread that he was finally going to run the mile, people came from everywhere to cheer him on. Finally, the moment came to start the event. Ike's coach came up to him and pushed Ike's left hand into his windbreaker's pocket, took out some tape, and taped it to his side. He then did the same to Ike's right hand. As a child, Ike had been stricken with polio, leaving his arms paralyzed. He was at a great disadvantage when it came to competing with students with healthy bodies. Nevertheless, his goal was to run the mile. As the gun cracked in the morning air, Ike took off running. There was tremendous applause for him as he came down to the last 100 yards of the race, approaching the finish line. The onlookers cheered every stride. Ike felt as though his lungs would burst and his legs would cramp and cause him to fall. But as he saw the line moving closer he reached back for all the reserve energy he could muster, then burst across the finish line, falling totally exhausted into the arms of his teammates. They grabbed him, threw him up onto their shoulders, held him high in the air, and circled the track. Did he win? Yes, sure he did. Did he come in first? No. Everyone else in the event crossed the finish line before he did, yet he was a winner because he ran with all he had.

I often wonder why when it comes to the highway of holiness we are so haphazard, so nominal, so casual and indifferent. How are you running this race? Are you running with excellence? Are you an encouragement to others as you run? Are you attempting to persuade every person you encounter to run the race with you? As people watch you run along this highway, what do they see? Do they encounter exuberance or a stiff, long face? This is the only way that leads to eternal life. The other option is the road that leads to destruction, banished forever from the presence of God. What a contrast! Who are you taking with you?

10

Works of Grace

I am often asked, "Why two distinct works of grace?" and "Why do you complicate things by talking about being saved and then subsequently sanctified?"

I believe the case for two distinct works of grace is supported by theology, opinions, and claims of many brilliant biblical scholars. One must also consider the tens of thousands of testimonies of persons who claim the reality of God's sanctifying grace as it followed their salvation.

To understand the doctrine of entire sanctification, it is helpful to have a fundamental understanding that the New Testament was written for new Christians. Paul directed his first letter to Thessalonica to a congregation of people who were believers in "the Lord Jesus Christ" (1 Thess. 1:1).

They were His followers, they had been transformed, and they were endeavoring to live for Christ and faithfully serve Him. Paul, as their leader, was concerned for their spiritual welfare. He encourages them with these words: "May God himself, the God of peace, sanctify you through and through" (5:23). The letter is not written to the unbeliever but to the believer.

While it is certain that much of the New Testament was written to the unsaved, the majority of texts were written to the believing Body of Christ. For instance, all of the Epistles were written either to individual believers or to congregations of believers. The New Testament does not urge unsaved people to be sanctified. Rather, it urges the unsaved to repent of their sins and be justified—to believe in Jesus Christ as their personal Savior (see Acts 16:29-31). Just as a person cannot be both hot and cold at the same time, the predominant indication of the New Testament is that a believer is not both saved and sanctified in the same experience.

Second, it seems logical that you have to be born before you can be cleansed. The unsaved person is spiritually dead. When you are born again you have "crossed over from death to life" (John 5:24) immediately and become a new person in Christ. You are a candidate for all of the other gifts God has for His children, including His sanctifying grace. It's just like the precious newborn infant after it is delivered and ready to be cleaned up and grow!

I believe persons are more confused about the timing between salvation and sanctification than they are about whether or not it exists as two distinct works of grace. Several persons responded to an invitation I gave at the conclusion of my message in one particular church. One of them was the pastor's 11- or 12-year-old son. Before we prayed he told me he was a backslider and wanted to be forgiven. Together we asked God to forgive his sin and bring him back into a right relationship with his Heavenly Father. When I looked at him, he assured me that God had forgiven him. I continued praying with others who had come to the altar when, a while later, I looked in his direction and saw that he was praying again, this time with even greater intensity. As soon as I was able to return to pray with him, I asked, "Is there something wrong? Didn't you feel like you were really saved a few moments ago?" He assured me that he was saved but explained that if he was ever going to live the kind of life he knew God had for him and be a strong witness for Christ at school, he needed to be sanctified. He continued to explain that he thought the reason for his backsliding was that he had never been sanctified. He affirmed that he was not going to leave the altar this time without knowing that God had also sanctified him! He remained in earnest prayer for quite a while, and eventually stood up with a profession of being saved and sanctified!

I believe you must be alive in Christ (see Eph. 2:5). You must cross over "from death to life" (John 5:24). It doesn't matter how much or how little time passes between the two works of salvation and sanctification. The interval of time will be different just as each believer is different. For some it may be a very short length of time as it was for the youngster I just told you about. For others it might be months or years between salvation and sanctification.

Time is not the only elemental shift between the distinction of salvation and sanctification. I believe there are two distinct conditions of sin that must be dealt with, making it necessary for two distinct works of grace.

We are born with a sinful disposition for which we are not responsible. However, we *are* responsible for the effect our sin nature has on our spiritual lives. Because Adam and Eve brought this sin upon us by their disobedience to God, the guilt is theirs. However, because of this spiritual pollution, we are inclined to disobey God's best plan for us and do things our own way.

Do you remember throwing tantrums, yelling

at your brothers and sisters, telling lies? Those are willful sins and, sorry, but you're responsible for those. They may have been part of our human nature, but it is our responsibility to ask God to forgive us for those sins. And He will! When we ask Him to forgive us, every act of sin we have ever committed is forgiven—and we are born again.

But the inherited nature that causes us to be *inclined* to these behaviors is something different. At some point after we begin a new relationship with Jesus Christ we become aware that we still have a *leaning* toward sin. Our hearts are still in conflict with the spirit of Christ within us. We still battle self-interests, selfish ambitions, and self-centeredness. The only solution for this condition is total consecration to God. The Holy Spirit must cleanse our hearts, resulting in entire sanctification. At that point our hearts are free from the *disease* of sin, and Christ is truly Lord of our lives.

Remember, there is nothing about entire sanctification that removes our humanity. We can be both holy and human at the same time. As newly sanctified children of God we experience the normal drives, hungers, and desires of humans. We will be tempted to fulfill those desires in ways contradictory to God's plan for our lives. But we have the power of personal choice, and God does not remove that free choice because of our new relationship with Him. If He did, we would be puppets.

There is always the possibility in our spiritual walks that we will come to a point of temptation when we choose to sin by making a wrong choice. I don't believe we ever reach a point in this life where it is impossible to sin. But I do believe that it is possible to resist temptation and live a victorious Christian life. Through the power of the Holy Spirit we can say no to sin and live a pure, consistent, and victorious Christian life. We recognize that it is possible to sin, and should it happen to us, "We have one who speaks to the Father in our defense" (1 John 2:1). Jesus was tempted, yet His heart remained pure. To think that because a person's heart is pure he or she will never be tempted again is not realistic nor is it scriptural. Don't settle for anything less than a triumphant spiritual life!

If you are a high-strung, emotional person before sanctification, you will still be high-strung and emotional after sanctification. If you are mild-mannered and calm, you will remain mild-mannered and calm. Don't plan to join the choir after you are sanctified if you can't carry a tune in a bucket!

We humans are by nature self-centered and selfish. When the Holy Spirit enters our lives we become Christ-centered and others-centered. We will no longer insist on having everything our way—although we may still prefer it.

To think that a sanctified person will never experience anger is unrealistic. Remember that people and circumstances even angered Jesus when He was on earth. But from His example we can learn that it is our reaction to people and circumstances that changes after we are sanctified. We are made of flesh and blood and our bodies are equipped to handle only so much stress, anxiety, depression, moodiness, and exhaustion. When we feel these things we will be more keenly aware of our need for rest, a change of pace, or a change of scenery. It is important to realize the limitations of our minds and bodies.

Is there a need for repentance in the sanctified walk? Yes! Entire sanctification does not give us perfect patience and poise, although we will begin to develop more patience, forgiveness, and a kinder attitude to those around us. Sanctification is both a crisis of consecration and cleansing as well as a process of becoming more Christlike as we grow in our newfound grace. Each day, month, and year will find us kinder, more loving, and more patient as we mature. And when we stumble and fail, God is gracious to forgive when we ask Him.

For seven years I served as executive director of the Christian Holiness Association. My wife, Ella Mae, was my secretary. Each year during the annual convention, we checked into the hotel on

Sunday evening and did not check out until Monday of the following week, having never left the building. It was a grueling week of long days and short nights. I remember one incident in particular. Ella Mae and I had just returned to our room at about two o'clock in the morning. Everyone else had gone to bed, but we were still finishing a couple of tasks before we could call it a day. I asked Ella Mae if she had taken care of something I had asked her to do that morning. "Oh," she exclaimed. "I completely forgot."

I couldn't believe it! It was important, she forgot it, and I was upset. I confess that I spoke unkindly to her. As soon as I did it, she turned toward her desk so I couldn't see her face.

Immediately I felt convicted and thought, *Hermiz, you couldn't pay anyone else to work these kinds of hours! You've been unkind to her because she forgot to do something. You are wrong and you need to apologize.*

I walked over to the desk where she was working and turned her around to find a tear trickling down her cheek. I brushed the tear aside and said, "Please forgive me. I shouldn't have spoken that way. I was wrong, and I'm sorry. Please forgive me."

Humility is a part of the holy life. There will be times when you will need to apologize. As you grow spiritually it will be not just a matter of saying you're sorry but also a matter of how quickly you sense when you are wrong and that you need to make it right. That will be an indication of your close walk with God and your genuine love for Him.